Ray Charles

Ray Charles

Soul Man

Ruth Turk

Lerner Publications Company • Minneapolis

*To my editor at Lerner Publications, Becka McKay,
with warm appreciation for constructive criticism
and understanding*

Library of Congress Cataloging-in-Publication Data

Turk, Ruth.
    Ray Charles : soul man / by Ruth Turk.
      p.   cm.
    Includes bibliographical references (p.   ) and index.
    Summary: A biography of the popular singer, who became blind as a
young boy.
    ISBN 0-8225-4928-X (alk. paper)
    1. Charles, Ray 1930–   —Juvenile literature. 2. Singers—United States—
Biography—Juvenile literature. [1. Charles, Ray, 1930–   . 2. Singers.
3. Afro-Americans—Biography. 4. Blind.]
    ML3930.C443T87   1996
    782.42164'092—dc20
    [B]   95-20953

Manufactured in the United States of America
1 2 3 4 5 6 – JR – 00 01 99 98 97 96

CONTENTS

From the time he was a little boy, Ray Charles Robinson loved to play Mr. Pit's piano.

BEFORE THE DARKNESS

ON A STIFLING, HOT SUMMER DAY IN THE LITTLE town of Greenville, Florida, Aretha Robinson told her four-year-old son, Ray, to stay in the shade. As the sound of piano music floated on the breeze toward him, however, the small boy forgot his mother's words. Scarcely feeling the hot sunshine on his head, he skipped excitedly down the road, listening as the wonderful sound grew louder and louder. When Ray got to the Red Wing Café, he pushed open the door and went in. He knew he didn't need an invitation. Wylie Pitman, the owner, was a kind and friendly man who always treated Ray like his very own son.

The Red Wing Café was a small general store that sold beer, soda, tobacco, and other items to Greenville's black community. To Ray the most important thing was the rickety old piano that stood in the middle of the cafe. Seeing Mr. Pit—as Ray called him—sitting at the piano, the boy climbed up beside him on the bench. His eyes grew wide with fascination as he watched the man's fingers race up and down the keys. When Mr. Pit was finished, he smiled into the small, upturned face. Reaching over, he took Ray's small fingers, placed them on the keys, and showed him how to play.

This was the first of many afternoons Ray spent with Mr. Pit. Wylie Pitman was a patient and caring teacher who understood Ray's love of music.

Born on September 23, 1930, Ray Charles Robinson grew up in Greenville, 30 miles south of the Georgia border. Though on maps the town's name read Greenville, those who lived there, black or white, always pronounced it "Greensville" with an s. Greenville was a tiny rural community. Black people lived in one area and white people lived in another. White children and black children attended separate schools. Blacks and whites did not mix socially, in church, or any other way. Ray did not know that the separation of the races was called segregation. He thought it was a normal way of life, and in childhood he did not question it.

Ray Charles was not born blind. As a young child he was able to see everything around him. He loved the colors of nature in the country, the sun, the moon, and the stars. His parents, Aretha and Bailey Robinson, were very poor, but Ray and his little brother, George, didn't realize

In a typical small town in the Deep South in the 1930s, a man gets a haircut in front of a store.

it. They didn't always have shoes to wear, but they always had plenty of delicious home-cooked food to eat.

Ray and George were happy kids. They played in the woods near their tiny shack. They played games, threw pebbles in the stream, and picked blackberries, but they never strayed far from the sound of their mother's voice warning them to watch out for rattlesnakes.

The boys received a lot of care and affection from their mother. "Mama" was Ray's birth mother, Aretha. Ray also spent a lot of time at the house of his father's first wife, Mary Jane, whom he called "Mother." Mary Jane's only

child had died as a baby, and she spoiled Ray as if he
were her own son. Bailey Robinson, Ray's father, was
away from home most of the time, working as a railroad
repairman. Mama and Mother both worked hard to make
up for his absence.

Though Aretha and Mary Jane were quite different
from each other, they got along well. Aretha worked in
the tobacco and cotton fields and took in washing and

*Ray's mother worked in the fields of northern Florida, painted here
by Jules Andre Smith.*

A rural Baptist church in the Deep South. Ray loved to hear the music and sing at church.

ironing when she was home. Mary Jane had a job at the sawmill in town and cleaned the houses of rich white families. Aretha was strict with her boys and insisted that they follow certain rules, while Mary Jane was more lenient. Sometimes Mother managed to persuade Mama not to whip Ray when he was naughty. Mother's pet name for the young boy was "monkey doodle."

Sunday was an important day for Ray because he could hear the music and join in the singing at the local Baptist church. Mama would wake up Ray and George very early, but Ray didn't object. He was always anxious to get out of bed for music.

In addition to the piano at the Red Wing Café, the old jukebox that stood in a corner of the cafe provided Ray with many pleasant hours. Without the jukebox, Ray might never have become familiar with the sounds of blues and boogie-woogie music so early in his life.

Sometimes Ray took his little brother along to the cafe. Ray and George were best pals. George was a year younger, but he was very smart for his age. By the time he was three years old, he could already add, multiply, and divide. Mama didn't have enough money for store-bought games and toys, so George put together all sorts of things with strings and wires. He made little cars and trucks that he and Ray played with for hours.

One afternoon, while Mama was inside the house ironing, the two brothers ran out to play in the backyard. Since the day was hot and sunny, George and Ray thought they would cool off by splashing in the big tub of rinse water Mama kept in the yard. After a while, Ray got tired of splashing and climbed out. George kept on kicking and hopping up and down, yelling for his brother to come back. Suddenly, the splashing and yelling stopped. Turning around, Ray saw that his little brother's head was underwater. Ray jumped into the tub and tried to yank the small body out, but his five-year-old arms weren't strong enough. He screamed for Mama with all his might. She came running out and jumped into the tub to pull

George out. She bent over his tiny body and breathed into his mouth. She kept blowing air and slapping his back, but it was too late. Ray's little brother was dead.

Ray watched his mother's tears spill down her face, but his own eyes were dry. All kinds of scary thoughts kept racing through his head, but he couldn't cry. He had loved his brother so much—why couldn't he have saved him?

The sudden death of his brother was Ray's first experience with tragedy. It was also one of the last things he would ever see clearly. A few months later, Ray's eyes started giving him trouble. A strange, thick liquid began to ooze out of the corners of his eyes. He tried to wipe it away with his fingers, but everything looked dim and blurry. Ray was too young to understand what was happening, but in her heart, Mama realized that her son now stood at the beginning of a dark and lonely road.

Separated from the black children, white children at the Florida School for the Deaf and Blind make brooms and cane chairs.

SCHOOL FOR THE BLIND

RAY DID NOT LOSE HIS EYESIGHT ALL AT ONCE. IT happened gradually. When he woke up in the mornings, his eyelids were pasted tight together. Mama would gently apply a cool, damp cloth until Ray could open his eyes, but everything still looked hazy and blurred, like a painting left out in the rain. Ray had always loved bright colors. Now the brilliant blue of the sky and the fresh green of the grass grew dimmer day by day. At night he could scarcely pick out the stars twinkling in the sky.

Mama took Ray to one of the two doctors in Greenville who would see black patients. Dr. McCloud treated Ray's eyes with drops and ointments, but nothing helped his condition. Finally the doctor advised Mama to take Ray to a clinic in the nearby town of Madison. After a long examination, the clinic doctor told Mama some bad news. Her six-year-old son was going blind. He had glaucoma. In 1936 there was not enough medical knowledge

15

available to successfully treat this disease. In most cases, increasing pressure inside the eyeballs led to total loss of vision, and this was happening to Ray.

As soon as Aretha knew that nothing could be done to save her son's eyesight, she tried to find out if there were special schools for blind children. Her own education had ended in fifth grade, and she knew how important it was for her son to be well educated. She couldn't do anything to prevent Ray's blindness, but she was determined he would learn to read and write. Aretha knew that it was vital for Ray to be independent and able to take care of his own needs for the rest of his life.

Aretha asked everyone in town about special schools. When she learned about the Florida School for the Deaf and Blind in St. Augustine, she applied for Ray immediately. Ray was accepted for the following term. Mama told him he would soon have to leave home.

If he could have, Ray would have bawled like a baby, but crying hurt his eyes too much. He wasn't ready to leave home or the two people he loved most in the world—Mama and Mary Jane. Ray pleaded with his mother to let him stay with her. The thought of riding on a train to a strange place 160 miles away was terrifying. Mary Jane didn't want Ray to leave, either, but Mama stuck to her guns. Ray might be only six years old, but she believed he had to face what was happening to him.

Gently she explained to Ray that she might not always be around to help him. She felt that her own lack of education would only hinder Ray's progress. When the unhappy boy continued his pleas, Aretha would not discuss it any further.

Ray had only a few months to get used to the idea of leaving home. During this period, Mama redoubled her efforts to make her son as independent as possible. She insisted he wash and dress himself and carry out chores such as washing dishes, scrubbing floors, and chopping wood. Ray still went over to Mr. Pit's place whenever he could, climbing up on the piano stool and running his small fingers across the keys. Mr. Pit encouraged Ray and taught him what he knew. Sometimes Mr. Pit allowed Ray to ride in his old car, showing him how to steer, shift gears, and apply the brakes. With so much love and caring surrounding him, it was no wonder young Ray didn't want to leave home. Nevertheless, in September 1937, now able to see only shadows and faint outlines, Ray Charles Robinson arrived at the Florida School for the Deaf and Blind.

At first, he was very homesick. He missed Mama and Mary Jane and the woods he used to play in with his brother.

Most of the kids at the school seemed to know each other, but Ray kept to himself and didn't talk to anyone. He had never been away from home. He was in a strange environment, and his eyes kept hurting. The other kids thought he felt sorry for himself. They teased Ray and called him names. Even worse, because Mama did not have money to buy new clothes, he had to wear second-hand clothes that the school gave to the poorest children.

A postcard of the Florida School for the Deaf and Blind

Some of the kids had partial vision. They noticed Ray's appearance and made fun of him.

It took a while for Ray to discover that the school was divided into a black side and a white side. Black teachers taught the black students and white teachers taught the white students. The idea that children who couldn't see were separated from each other by color seemed strange, but Ray was too young and upset to think much about it at first.

Because Mama had been strict with Ray, adjusting to the new school routine was not as tough as it might have been. The day started at 5:30 A.M. with breakfast, followed by chapel and morning classes. After lunch there were more classes, workshops, a play period, then supper and a study period before bedtime. When Ray realized he was at the school to stay, he began to make the most of his hours and days there.

He learned to read and write in braille—a special alphabet that consists of raised dots on paper. Braille was invented in 1824 by Louis Braille, a French teacher who was blind himself. These dots are raised so blind people can feel them with their fingers and read the letters and

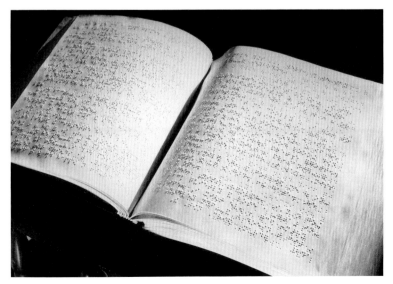

A braille book

words they represent. The dots can also be pressed out with a special machine so that blind people can write.

Ray learned the braille system faster than he expected. In a short time, he was able to read and write. The school had no library, but Ray managed to read some books he got in class. He enjoyed *The Adventures of Huckleberry Finn* and *The Adventures of Tom Sawyer* because they were about country life and reminded him of home.

During recess Ray played in the schoolyard with some of the other boys and became good at running. The children played a version of football that was almost like regular football, except without passing.

Ray also did well in workshop. He learned how to carve wood, how to weave cane for chair bottoms, and how to make things out of leather.

Ray soon discovered the school's music room. He spent whatever time he could spare listening to students practice on the piano. He knew he would be able to take music lessons the next year, when he turned eight. For now he did his best to be patient.

When Christmas rolled around, Ray looked forward to a visit home. He was stunned to find out that he would have to spend the Christmas holiday at school. No one had remembered to tell Ray that families had to pay for students' holiday transportation. Even if they had, Mama would not have had money for the trip. When Ray was all alone, he cried his heart out.

Never before had time dragged by as slowly as it did that Christmas vacation. When Ray had first arrived at the school, he'd been too shy to talk to anyone. By the time his schoolmates returned from vacation, he was so glad to hear their voices and the sound of running in the halls, he welcomed them back like dear, lifelong friends.

Although Ray had experienced pain in his eyes before, his right eye now throbbed and burned so much he could hardly bear it. When the doctor said the eye had to be removed, Ray was overcome with fear and panic. The thought of losing an eye actually seemed scarier than going blind. Ray had never had an operation before, and he didn't know what to expect. When it was over, Ray was happy to go home to be with Mama and Mary Jane. Less than a year before, Ray had still been able to see shadows. Now the darkness was complete. But as long as Ray could be with the people he loved, he felt there was still some light.

Ray grew up in a small, poor, rural community in northern Florida.

BLIND BUT NOT STUPID

WHEN RAY CAME HOME FOR THE SUMMER, MAMA was more determined than ever not to give him special treatment. Mama wanted Ray to be like the other kids. But the attitude of concerned neighbors who did not understand what she was doing sometimes made her task difficult.

For example, when she saw that Ray was confident about riding his bicycle, she let him ride a little farther from home every day. Ray loved the feeling of speed. He would not let blindness stop him from enjoying his bike. Listening intently to all the sounds around him, Ray skillfully maneuvered his bike on the paths and roads in and around Greenville. Ray's hearing and instincts became so keen that he never fell and hurt himself or his bike.

Watching Ray riding around town, neighbors started thinking that maybe Aretha Robinson had become indifferent to her son's welfare. Greenville was a tiny community, and Ray was the only blind child who lived there.

One day Mama took Ray out in the backyard and told him to chop wood for the fire. Two neighbors passing by stopped to watch. They couldn't believe their eyes. They scolded Aretha, asking how she could be so cruel to a small blind boy. Aretha did not get upset. She stood her ground and answered them.

"He's blind," she explained, "but he ain't stupid. He's lost his sight, but he ain't lost his mind."

Mama went back into the house, and Ray continued chopping wood. Mama had made up her mind she would raise her son to take care of himself, no matter what anyone said. Amazingly, Ray never did hurt himself, whether he was chopping wood, cooking, washing clothes, scrubbing floors, or cleaning fish. Ray was not especially fond of doing chores, but he understood that Mama had his best interests at heart. Her confidence gave him the kind of independence he might never have otherwise had.

Ray's second year in school was much better than the first. He found more friends. He was one of the few blind kids in the school who communicated with the deaf students there. He learned sign language so that his deaf friends could "speak" to him by tracing signs or letters in the palms of his hands. When Ray replied, they read his lips. Ray enjoyed this experience and was proud that he was good at it.

By the time he was eight years old, Ray had started taking regular music lessons. Even though he was young, he wanted more than anything else to become a great musician. At Mr. Pit's place, he had listened to every kind of popular music—jazz, blues, boogie-woogie—but in school he was only allowed to play classical music. While he felt a bit limited, Ray didn't really mind. All music fascinated him. When Ray was 11, he became the youngest student to join the school choir.

One of Ray's favorite activities was listening to the radio. The school had only one radio. The oldest boys always decided what the others would hear. During the 1940s, big-band music was the most popular sound on the

In the 1940s, Ray listened to the big-band sounds of Benny Goodman, lower right, *and his band on the radio.*

radio. Ray enjoyed the music of the great band leaders such
as Glenn Miller, Tommy Dorsey, Glen Gray, and Benny
Goodman. When he heard the clarinet played by band
leader Artie Shaw, Ray fell in love with the elegant
sound. He started to take clarinet lessons.

By the time he was 12, Ray began to venture off the
school grounds. Gradually he moved around the streets
and roads, exploring by himself, just as he had back in
Greenville. He was determined not to be dependent on a
cane or a guide dog. He did not want to be considered
helpless. Instead, he would have someone escort him to
the unfamiliar parts of town. There, Ray used his ears to
remember the particular steps, twists, and turns of the
area. Soon he became comfortable enough with each new
place to venture there on his own. "No dog, no cane, no
guitar. There was never a time when I didn't believe I
could do what I was trying to do."

During the next few years, Ray continued to spend as
much time as he could possibly manage playing one of
the school's three pianos. Sometimes he sneaked in his
playing after hours, when the teachers weren't around.
Because the music department taught only classical music, Ray thought they wouldn't approve of the jazz and
blues he liked to experiment with. Sometimes other kids
joined him at the piano and jumped and danced around
in time to the beat.

Ray's music teacher arranged for him to play at tea parties and other social occasions for women's clubs in St.
Augustine. Being able to go off campus and entertain a

group of people was new and exciting. The idea of becoming a real performer was appealing and challenging. Ray played popular songs that the women liked. It felt good to hear them humming along in time to the music. Most of the time, Ray did not receive payment for his performance, but he really didn't mind. Once in a while, an audience collected a small sum of money to give him, or they treated him to fresh fruit and candy.

In addition to entertaining and singing in the choir, Ray organized some of his friends into a small informal singing group. The more Ray listened to popular singers, the more he tried to imitate their different sounds, just to see if he could—and he usually could.

One singer in particular influenced Ray more than others—Nat Cole. Cole also played the piano, and Ray just couldn't get enough of Cole's special style of music. His deep romantic voice and the smooth, easy way he accompanied himself was so inspiring that before long he became Ray's idol. Not only did Ray listen to every number Cole sang on the radio, but he also spent hours imitating everything the singer did.

As a result of studying Nat Cole's style so intently, Ray began to sound like him. Songs that were popular in the 1940s, such as "Straighten Up and Fly Right" and "All for You" became part of Ray's repertoire. He thought that by imitating Cole's style he would be able to gain popularity and recognition for himself. Though Ray was not ready to develop an original sound, he was gradually building the confidence he needed to be a professional musician.

Ray didn't question the fact that blacks and whites were segregated in Greenville.

CHAPTER FOUR

A TERRIBLE LOSS

OVER THE NEXT FEW YEARS, RAY SETTLED INTO the routine of going home in the summer and returning to school in the fall. Being away from home was no longer the hardship it had been in the beginning, but spending the summer months at home was the best vacation he could have asked for. Ray felt like he belonged in Greenville, where he knew most of his neighbors. In Greenville, Ray's favorite people, Mama and Mary Jane, were always there for him.

Greenville was a segregated community, but Ray had little notion of what segregation really meant. The fact that white people and black people lived apart from each other and used different public facilities was something Ray accepted without questioning. Sometimes his father's mother, Grandmother Margaret Robinson, told Ray stories of the days of slavery. Muh, as she was called, had been a slave herself. She would describe vividly how slaves were mistreated by their white masters. While Ray believed her, he did not take these tales very seriously.

A couple named Henry and Alice Johnson owned a café in another part of Greenville. Ray spent many hours listening to the café's jukebox. Sometimes a customer would give Ray money to buy ice cream or candy, but Ray put the nickels in the jukebox instead. Listening to music was far more exciting for him than eating sweets. Like Mr. Pit, Henry Johnson let Ray drive his car. He would sit beside Ray and give him directions.

When the Johnsons moved to Tallahassee, Florida— about 50 miles east of Greenville—Ray visited them. In Tallahassee, Mr. and Mrs. Johnson opened another café and became active in the black church community. When the Johnsons learned that Ray loved to play the clarinet but didn't have one of his own, they convinced the church elders to raise money to buy one for their young friend.

Having a shiny new clarinet of his own was a dream come true. Ray carried it around as if it were part of him. Alice Johnson also saw to it that Ray had enough clothes and even the special foods he liked.

Ray was an outgoing teenager who had no difficulty making friends wherever he went. He liked to hang out at a grocery store down the block from the Johnsons' home. The owner, Mr. Bison, had a daughter named Lucille, who had the run of the store. As she got to know Ray better, Lucille let Ray use the cash register. He rang up sales and made change for the customers. This job gave him a lot of confidence and he treasured the experience.

Ray visited the Johnsons in Tallahassee.

When Ray was 14, he learned to ride a motorcycle that had been lent to him by a friend. Ray loved racing up and down the streets and hills of Greenville, usually close beside his friend or next to him. The sound of the other motorcycle's exhaust was enough to guide Ray.

It was hard to believe that a blind person could ride a motorcycle without having a serious accident, but Ray had tremendous confidence in his ability. Some strangers saw Ray riding one day and, not believing he was blind, reported him to the authorities. Since Ray received state money to attend the school for the blind, he had to report for an eye exam to prove he was blind. After the exam confirmed Ray's blindness, he went out and climbed right back on his motorcycle.

One summer in Tallahassee, Ray met a musician named Cannonball Adderley, who played in the popular Florida A & M College band. Through Adderley, Ray was able to sit in with the group and play piano. Florida A & M was the first big band Ray had ever played with, and he felt proud. When he returned home and Mama heard about it, she was proud of him too, but she didn't hesitate to put her son in his place.

Cannonball Adderley

One day Mama caught Ray smoking. She punished him by making him smoke the entire pack of cigarettes right then. Ray felt like he was going to choke to death.

Another time Mama put two fat sweet potatoes in the fireplace to roast. Then she went out of the room, leaving Ray alone. Soon Ray smelled the delicious aroma of the roasting potatoes. He just couldn't wait for Mama to return and give him permission to have one. Instead, reaching into the fire, he grabbed a potato and pulled it out. Just then Mama came back into the room. Without thinking, Ray stuffed the hot potato into his pocket. As the fierce heat began to burn his skin, he started to jump up and down and hop from one leg to the other. Mama waited quietly. Ray finally dug the hot potato out of his pocket and put it back into the fireplace. Mama reminded Ray that stealing would get him "burned" as surely as the hot potato. If he wanted something, he would have to ask.

At age 14, Ray thought that life at school was moving too slowly. The regular lessons were easy for him. He was usually able to do the homework from one class while sitting in another. He started hanging around with some older kids because they were in the school band. Ray became fascinated by the idea of writing arrangements— music for an entire band. He learned how to compose parts for all the instruments and make them blend. After a while, he was able to call out notes to another musician, who would write them down.

At school, Ray learned to play games like dominoes
and cards. He invented his own method of brailling the
cards. When he discovered an old Underwood type-
writer, he taught himself to type and sent letters home.
But if a piano was anywhere around, Ray was pretty sure
to be found in front of it. Back home in Greenville, white
and black neighbors alike let Ray play their musical instruments and were rewarded with fabulous music.

In May 1945, while Ray was in school, he received
some shocking news that called him home to Greenville.
Mama had died from a sudden attack of food poisoning.
Neither the drowning of his little brother nor his own
blindness seemed as terrible to Ray as his mother's death.
It felt like the end of the world. Ray's mother used to warn
him that someday she would be gone, but now that she
was, he didn't know how to accept living without her.

For more than a week, Ray wandered around in a
trance. He didn't pray. He didn't cry. There was a lump in
his throat like a rock that wouldn't go away. He didn't eat
or sleep. Ray knew that people were worried about him,
but he could not communicate. The more he kept his
feelings bottled up inside, the worse they became.

He couldn't stop thinking of how unfair it was—Mama
was only 32 years old. Ray hadn't seen her since Christmas. He wondered if she had known how much he'd
loved her.

Mr. Pit and the Johnsons tried hard to comfort the

grieving boy. Mary Jane was there to console him, but nobody had been as close to Ray as Mama. For a while, Ray thought he was going to lose his mind. He kept longing to hear his mother's voice and to kiss her one more time.

Finally a Greenville woman called Ma Beck came to see Ray. Ma Beck had a reputation in the town as a special person who had the remarkable gift of helping troubled people heal themselves. Ma Beck looked straight into the eyes of the grief-stricken boy and spoke to him gently but firmly. She told him that his Mama wouldn't want him to be acting this way. She told him to remember what Mama had tried to teach him and to stop feeling sorry for himself. Finally Ma Beck said that Ray must carry on, because that would have been his mother's wish.

Suddenly Ray fell into Ma Beck's arms and began to sob. He stayed there for a long time, crying out all the pain and anguish. Ma Beck held him gently. She did not say another word.

Ray was ready to go to his mother's funeral and mourn with relatives, friends, and neighbors. As he stood in the graveyard, he listened to the sounds of weeping and praying. He remembered how Mama told him not to beg or steal and to believe that he could do whatever he had to do. She had warned him if he didn't have faith in himself he would sink to the bottom.

In that moment, Ray realized he must not let himself sink. He had to face whatever the future had in store, and face it the way his Mama had wanted. Ray was 15 years old. The only way to go was forward.

After Mama died, Ray moved to Jacksonville and stayed with friends of Mary Jane's.

C H A P T E R   F I V E

MOVING ON

In the weeks following Mama's passing, Ray realized he would have to make a decision about staying in school. He didn't ask advice from his friends because he didn't want them to feel sorry for him. If he asked the preacher or the doctor who knew him, they would probably tell him to return to school. Ray wasn't sure that was what he wanted to do.

The easiest thing would be to stay in the state school, where all his needs would be taken care of. Mary Jane offered him a home with her for as long as he wanted, but Ray was determined not to become a burden to anyone. He was curious about what other places in Florida and the rest of the country were like. When Mary Jane contacted friends who lived in Jacksonville, they invited the teenager to come and stay with them. Ray agreed, but only if he could help with expenses.

Lena Mae and Fred Thompson treated the 15-year-old more like a son than a boarder. Ray slept in his own room off the kitchen and had to come home at a certain time or let the Thompsons know where he would be. Since Ray was accustomed to Mama's rules and regulations, this was not a problem for him. He knew that Lena Mae and Fred were looking out for him because they cared.

Whenever Ray made a few dollars playing the piano at parties in Jacksonville, he would buy some food at the grocery store and leave it on the Thompsons' kitchen table. This food was the only kind of payment that the couple would accept from Ray.

Jacksonville was the first big city Ray had ever lived in, but he learned to get around by himself as soon as possible. Before he left Greenville, a group of white residents had offered to buy Ray a Seeing Eye dog—a specially trained guide dog for the blind—but he turned down the offer. While he appreciated the kind thought, he felt that relying on an animal to lead him around would take away the independence he valued. In Jacksonville, Fred took Ray places first, and in his usual manner, Ray learned the routes by heart.

When Ray learned that there was a musicians' union— Local 632—down the street from his new home, the first thing he did was join. He knew he could probably earn a living as a mechanic or a carpenter because he was good with his hands, but he was determined to be a professional musician. Being in the union would bring him into the company of other musicians, help him to find work at decent wages, and help him enter the music world.

Ray discovered a piano in the union meeting room and started coming in early before union meetings so he could play. Some of the union members heard him and started paying attention—exactly what Ray had hoped for. Soon other musicians around town heard about the young piano player. Ray let it be known that he was available to perform, even if just for his supper. He was willing to play anything—blues, jazz, boogie-woogie, or swing. He started getting calls to play gigs—professional engagements—around the city of Jacksonville.

The first big band Ray played with was Henry Washington's band, which consisted of 16 or 17 musicians. They played in nightclubs, theaters, and dance halls. Ray wasn't hired as their regular pianist, but he was thrilled to be called to sit in from time to time. Ray shouldn't have even been allowed inside some of the nightclubs because he was under the legal drinking age. But often, club managers liked the young musician enough to let him perform anyway. While he didn't make much money from these occasional gigs, the experience itself was worth a great deal to him.

Ray began to find himself in an adult world, growing up fast. He moved from place to place by himself, usually walking or taking a taxi. The musicians Ray met were considerably older than he was, and Ray liked playing with them in nightclubs until after midnight.

Though Ray had taken piano and clarinet instruction at school, he had never had a voice lesson. Yet he sang every song with feeling. As he saw it, there were two general types of sound. "Race records" had a moaning, low sound, performed by black artists such as Elmore James,

Muddy Waters, left, *and his band*

Tampa Red, and Muddy Waters. The other kind of sound—swing—had a bouncier, more upbeat feeling. Swing was more common on the radio, performed by white musicians such as Artie Shaw and Benny Goodman, as well as black musicians such as Count Basie and Duke Ellington. A little of every kind of music he heard influenced Ray's own playing, even the classical music by Bach, Beethoven, and Mozart that he had heard and played in school.

A band leader named Tiny York invited Ray to do a few gigs with him in central Florida. Unfortunately, the job fell through, and Ray found himself stranded in Orlando. He didn't blame York. By now Ray understood that the music world was sometimes unreliable. But Ray was running out of money, and there was no work in sight. He could have gone back to the Thompsons in Jacksonville, but he didn't want to depend on someone else for support. He was 16 years old and needed to hold on to his hard-won independence even when things got tough.

In Orlando, Ray found a kind-hearted woman who rented him a room. When he could scrape together the money, he paid her three or four dollars a week. Sometimes for supper Ray would have just a can of sardines with crackers, washed down with a glass of water. Other times, more than a day would pass before Ray ate anything. Gigs were scarce, and competition among musicians was fierce. Ray toured Orlando's nightclubs, searching for any playing job he could find. Once in a while, a gig would materialize and keep Ray from starvation. His natural stamina and determination pulled him through these hard times.

Ray got a real break when he met bandleader Joe Anderson. When Anderson found out that Ray could write arrangements, he asked Ray to do original arrangements for his band. Ray couldn't believe his luck. Nobody had ever asked him to do arrangements before. He was so delighted he forgot to ask Anderson to pay him!

During his stay in Orlando, Ray frequently had to cope

with hectic circumstances. Nightclubs usually had drinking and dancing, and sometimes customers got into nasty fights. Though Ray couldn't see punches exchanged or bottles flying through the air, he knew when to get out of the way. Often he found the nearest window and jumped out. He usually got a few bumps or bruises, but he figured they weren't as bad as what might have happened if he stayed.

In 1946 Lucky Millinder was big in the music business. Ray had been listening to Millinder's band for years. When someone suggested to Ray that he ought to get an audition with the bandleader, he jumped at the idea. A lot of people had been telling Ray how good he was, and he wanted to believe them.

Lucky Millinder agreed to give Ray an audition at his nightclub. Ray sang his best songs, played his best tunes, and tried hard to impress the bandleader. Afterward, he waited nervously for the verdict. But when Millinder spoke, Ray could not believe his ears. The bandleader told him he wasn't good enough. When Ray asked him what he meant, Millinder repeated the crushing statement in even plainer words.

"You heard me. You don't got what it takes."

The words came as a terrible blow. Lucky Millinder thought Ray had potential, but potential was not enough. The bandleader had high standards. Ray went back to his room and cried the rest of the day.

As soon as Ray earned a little money playing a few

gigs, he did something impractical. Even though he really needed the cash for food and rent, he went out and bought a record player. In the middle of the worst depression in his life, Ray needed the spiritual lift the record player provided. Listening to great performers such as Nat Cole, Lionel Hampton, Lester Young, Ella Fitzgerald, and Sara Vaughan, Ray felt more connected to the exciting music of the times. Ray especially loved to listen to Billie Holiday. People had told Ray that his voice carried the same sad quality as hers did.

Billie Holiday

Since work was scarce in Orlando, Ray took a bus 80 miles southwest to Tampa, Florida, where he met other musicians and made more friends. He played a few gigs in white nightclubs, where the song requests were different from those in black clubs. This difference helped expand Ray's repertoire. He also discovered the trick of making his voice sound deeper by working with a public-address system. As a young teenager, his voice had sounded too light, but as he grew older, it acquired more resonance. Ray could not be classified strictly as a tenor or a baritone—his wide vocal range enabled him to sing both high and low notes. Ray was developing a style that was all his own.

> ONCE THE MUSIC GOT STARTED IT WAS ALL FORGOTTEN— THERE'S SOMETHING ABOUT MUSIC THAT MAKES PEOPLE BACK UP IF THEY'RE COMING AT YOU.

In 1948 Ray got a job with a country-and-western band called the Florida Playboys. Most of the time he played the piano, but sometimes he got the opportunity to sing. He received between 15 and 20 dollars a night, more than he had ever earned.

Ray was the only black musician in the Florida Playboys. At the beginning of this job, Ray had concerns that some people might make fun of a blind black man playing country music. But he was accepted and received appreciative applause along with all the other musicians. Ray believed that as long as he entertained the customers with the music they wanted to hear, the color of his skin made no difference.

> We were playing all these weird places in small
> towns and they [the audience] couldn't figure me out.
> Everybody's white and then there I am. But I'll say
> one thing—once the music got started it was all for-
> gotten—there's something about music that makes
> people back up if they're coming at you.

By this time, Ray was quite aware of the segregation
practiced in the South. Traveling from place to place, he
had to deal with the indignities of separate rest rooms
and other segregated—and usually inferior—facilities for
black people. But he refused to let it disturb him. He tried
not to pay the situation a lot of attention.

After the gig was over, Ray left the country-and-western band and went his own way. Ray liked to be on his
own. Most of his attention was focused on making a living and becoming the best professional musician he
could be. For now, that meant traveling alone, and that
was all right with Ray.

Ray Charles began to wear dark glasses in the 1940s.

CHAPTER SIX

DARK GLASSES

IN THE LATE 1940S, TAMPA WAS A PRETTY BIG CITY, but 18-year-old Ray was comfortable moving from place to place on his own. He used the same procedure he always had: Someone walked him through the streets and around the buildings until he became familiar enough with them to find his way on his own. Ray was proud that he was able to move with as much confidence as people who had normal vision.

When some of his friends told him they thought he would look better in dark glasses, Ray decided to take the hint. His eyes always became teary and caked with matter, and he realized he looked better with his eyes covered up. He also invested in a black suit, black shoes, a white shirt, and black tie. This became the outfit he usually wore while performing.

One Sunday night, as Ray played the piano in a friend's living room, he met a young woman his age named Louise. Louise spoke to Ray in a soft, sweet voice. Ray felt an immediate attraction. He and Louise hit if off right away. They started seeing a great deal of each other and soon fell in love. When Louise's parents found out their daughter was dating a blind musician, they strongly objected. They did not believe a blind man could take care of their daughter in a responsible way.

Yet the more Louise's parents opposed the relationship, the stronger the young couple's attachment became. Louise came to Ray's gigs every night that he performed. During the days, they roamed the city hand in hand.

Tired of Louise's parents' objections, Louise and Ray decided to run away to Miami. Ray got a job in a nightclub. The couple rented a room and stayed for several weeks. Louise's parents kept calling, insisting that she come home.

Upset by so much pressure, Louise and Ray finally returned to Tampa, but things were not the same. Though Ray loved Louise, he was restless and unhappy. He was more confident than ever in his ability to perform, arrange, and write songs. But he was no longer content to stay in one place. There were other things to do and other places to explore. Most of the musicians he met came from distant cities like Chicago, New York, or St. Louis, and Ray had never even been out of the state of Florida. At 18, Ray had been on his own for three years. He was sure he could take care of himself wherever he was. The time had come to go exploring.

Ray had managed to save a few hundred dollars. He didn't know how far the money would get him, but he was impatient to find out. He called a musician friend of his, Gosady McGee, and asked him to bring over a map of the United States. McGee couldn't imagine why his friend wanted a map.

Ray asked him to find a big city on the map as far away from Tampa as possible but still within the United States. New York City was five inches from Tampa on the map, but Ray thought that New York City was too big. Los Angeles was seven inches away. Ray told his friend to find someplace even farther. McGee replied that, at eight inches from Tampa, Seattle must be the city Ray was looking for. Ray made up his mind that Seattle was where he wanted to go.

Ray didn't know anything about Seattle, but somehow it sounded mysterious and exciting. It was far away, and he wanted to see if he could make a living as a musician on his own. He promised Louise that he would send for her as soon as he could. Then he kissed her good-bye, packed a few clothes in a small suitcase, and boarded a bus to Seattle.

In 1948 Ray arrived in Seattle.

CHAPTER SEVEN

A Star
in Seattle

The bus trip to Seattle was long, hot, and boring. Ray had never spent so many hours on a bus. In 1948 segregation meant that Ray had to sit in the back of the bus with other black passengers. With his seat located directly over the motor, Ray was soon squirming and sweating like crazy. When the bus made a stop in Chicago, he went into the station. All he could find to eat at the segregated lunch counter was a stale sandwich.

At 5:00 A.M., weary and sore all over, Ray finally arrived in Seattle. He found a small hotel close to the bus station and fell immediately into bed. He slept for nearly 24 hours, scarcely knowing where he was. He woke up starving in the middle of the night and called the hotel desk to ask where he could find a place to eat. The desk clerk informed him that the only spot open at 3:00 A.M. was a nightclub called the Rocking Chair. A nightclub was not what Ray had in mind, but it was better than nothing.

Ray took a cab to the Rocking Chair. A husky guard at the entrance barred the way. He told Ray it was Talent Night—but that no one under age 21 was allowed.

Speaking fast and persuasively, Ray convinced the bouncer that he was a terrific talent who needed a break more than anything in the world. Once inside, Ray forgot about his hunger and waited for his turn to perform. Then he sat down at the piano and sang his heart out,

Ray sings his heart out.

performing an original number called "Drifting Blues." When he finished, the club rang with applause.

A few minutes later, someone approached Ray and asked if he could get a trio together to play at the local Elks Club that Friday night. Dizzy with hunger and excitement, Ray accepted immediately. He didn't have a trio—yet—but he was sure he could put one together. He couldn't believe his luck—he'd landed a job only one day after arriving in Seattle.

Ray's first Seattle gig happened in March 1948. It signaled the start of a new way of life for the young performer. He began to think of himself as an adult able to handle practically anything that came his way.

Ray formed a trio with two union members and delivered a successful performance for the Elks Club. When Gosady McGee—Ray's friend from Tampa—arrived in Seattle shortly after Ray, the two musicians decided to form a permanent group of their own. With McGee on guitar, another musician on bass, and Ray singing and playing the piano, they called themselves the McSon Trio ("Mc" from McGee and "Son" from Robinson). Ray decided to drop Robinson from his name. He didn't want to be confused with the boxer Sugar Ray Robinson. He also thought Ray Charles was an easier name to remember than Ray Robinson.

In only a few months, the McSon Trio was in demand all around Seattle. Ray and his group were hired by the Rocking Chair club, the Washington Social Club, the 908 Club, and others. These clubs attracted a sophisticated

The McSon Trio sang at the Black and Tan Club, right.

clientele of white as well as black patrons. The McSon
Trio frequently worked from midnight to 5:00 A.M. Ray
realized they were fast becoming a popular attraction.

In 1948, radio station KRSC in Seattle asked the McSon
Trio to play on the air. Hoping for new gigs, the trio gave
Gosady McGee's phone number over the air, which re-
sulted in an offer to appear on a television variety show
that ran for nearly six weeks. Not many people saw the

show, but it was the first of its kind that featured black performers.

The year 1948 brought other rewards. At the Rocking Chair, Ray met a man named Jack Lauderdale who liked Ray's musical style. Lauderdale owned a record company called Downbeat. Ray was thrilled when Lauderdale asked him to record an original song, "Confession Blues," that he had written back in Florida.

Ray sings in a recording session.

A few months later, Ray went to Los Angeles, where Downbeat was based. Ray recorded another original number, "Baby, Let Me Hold Your Hand." Ray was delighted when the song made the black charts and became a national hit. Black people were buying the record and becoming familiar with the name Ray Charles. Ray made very little money, however, because he knew nothing about publishing rights or royalties—the portion of the income paid to a composer or writer for his or her work.

Ray became very involved in the close-knit community of Seattle musicians and made a lot of friends. Among them was Quincy Jones, a teenage musician who played the trumpet and wanted to write jazz. The two musicians became friends, and Ray showed Quincy how he wrote for big bands.

A month or two after Ray settled in Seattle, he sent Louise a bus ticket to come and join him. They rented a small house and tried to set up housekeeping. At first things went smoothly. Louise cooked and cleaned and Ray went out to play his gigs. But problems soon began to emerge. Louise and Ray had all kinds of bills to pay, and when Ray was between jobs, they didn't always have enough money. Even though the two young people loved each other, tension began to build. Whenever they had a quarrel, Louise would run to the phone and call her mother. Living with someone else and being so far away from home were new experiences that Louise found hard to handle.

From the beginning, Louise's parents had been against

Ray, but now their feeling that the musician was not right for their daughter grew stronger. Louise's mother called Ray and insisted that he send her daughter home immediately. Ray refused and told the woman that if she wanted Louise to come home, she should send a bus ticket. A few days later, the bus ticket arrived in the mail.

Louise and Ray were hurt and upset. Louise was afraid that if she didn't go, her mother would come to get her. When Louise decided she had better leave, Ray was miserable. He hung around Seattle for a few weeks, then took off for Los Angeles to record some songs with Jack Lauderdale. While Ray was in Los Angeles, Louise tried to reach him to tell him she was pregnant, but she didn't know where he was.

In 1950 Ray's daughter Evelyn was born. A year later, Louise married someone else. Though their love affair was over, Ray kept in touch with his ex-sweetheart and supported his child.

Just as when he arrived, Ray was alone in Seattle.

As he experienced success in Seattle, Ray began to feel more confident of his talents.

CHAPTER EIGHT

CHANGING TIMES

RAY STARTED TO FEEL PRETTY GOOD ABOUT HIS accomplishments. He had come to Seattle as an unknown singer and now he had a steady gig at the popular Rocking Chair club. He had done radio and television appearances, and had won the attention of musicians and audiences alike. He was proud of himself.

But even though Ray knew many Seattle musicians on a professional level, he wanted to be a part of their social scene. He thought that while most of the performers respected his playing ability, they wouldn't invite him to their parties because of his age. Ray was young, but he didn't want to be left out. He wanted to be like everyone else.

Ray had never used drugs. But as he moved from one nightclub to another, he became aware of the sweet odor of marijuana. Ray was curious. When he discovered why some of the musicians went outside during their breaks, he asked if he could join them. At first they refused, but Ray wouldn't take no for an answer. He kept on bothering them until finally someone gave him a marijuana cigarette. Now Ray felt good because he was accepted by the crowd. A few months later, he tried heroin, a more powerful—and dangerous—drug. No one encouraged or pressured him. Ray just didn't want to miss out on an experience—good or bad.

Ray developed an addiction to drugs. In 1950 he was earning enough to pay his bills and to send money to Louise for Evelyn. But once he got hooked, his earnings had to cover the cost of drugs as well.

The mystery surrounding drugs made them even more intriguing to Ray. Because many of the musicians he admired were on drugs, he was curious to find out whether taking drugs made them perform better. Young and inexperienced, Ray tried to convince himself that getting "high" was desirable and that he could control his habit. But he did not realize how dangerously addictive heroin could be.

Ever since Ray had left school, he had always been on his own. He was particularly proud of the fact that, no matter how hard times were, he would never beg or even borrow money from anyone. Plenty of people wanted to help him simply because he was blind, but Ray could not bear to be pitied. He always wanted to be his own person, go where he wanted, and get there without being led by the hand. And once he was tired of a place, it was time to move on. In 1950 Ray thought that maybe Los Angeles might offer more opportunities. Ray took his trio with

In 1950 Ray moved to Los Angeles.

him, but they soon discovered there weren't many gigs
for a trio. The group decided to break up, but there were
no hard feelings. Ray's friends went back to Seattle.

Ray started hanging around Jack Lauderdale's office.
Lauderdale had a secretary named Loretta who liked the
young musician from Seattle. She offered him a place to
stay in her home. Besides solving Ray's housing problem,
this new relationship helped to soften the memory of losing Louise.

Jack and his girlfriend, Betty, frequently double-dated
with Ray and Loretta. Knowing Ray's passion for driving,
sometimes Jack would let Ray drive his car, while Jack sat
beside him, guiding Ray in the right direction.

Ray met a number of important people in the music
world. He was impressed by Art Tatum, a well-known
piano player. As Ray listened to Tatum perform, he wondered if he might have accomplished more on the piano
himself had he not branched out into singing, composing,
and arranging. For a short while, Ray considered giving
up composing and arranging to concentrate on singing
and playing.

Soon after he moved to Los Angeles, Ray headed out
on the road with a star performer named Lowell Fulson.
Fulson played the electric guitar and sang. Sponsored by
Jack Lauderdale, Fulson had a blues band that traveled
all around the country. As the headliner, Lowell Fulson's
act opened and closed the show. Ray would play the

Ray sings the blues.

piano and sing a few songs before intermission. He received 35 dollars a night.

The money was enough to take care of all Ray's needs, including what he spent on drugs. Fulson soon allowed Ray to take over as musical director whenever the bandleader wanted to play his guitar or sing the blues himself. Ray took this opportunity to do original arrangements for

the band. Ray was so elated to hear the instruments playing the notes he had written that he never charged Fulson
for any of the arrangements.

In the weeks that followed, Fulson's band traveled
throughout the Southwest, stopping in New Mexico,
Texas, and other places new to Ray. Sometimes on a Sunday morning in New Orleans or Dallas, he would be
awakened by the singing of a church gospel group that
happened to be practicing in the same hotel. Not shy, Ray
would follow the sound of the music and tap on the door.
As soon as he introduced himself, he was invited to join
in singing with the church group. Ray loved these encounters. Though he was now playing jazz and blues,
church music was the music of his childhood.

Not all of Ray's experiences on the road were pleasant.
As a youngster, he had not been very aware of racial prejudice. Touring big and small cities all around the country
with a black band exposed him to some of the shocking
and humiliating practices of segregation.

When the band performed in Myrtle Beach, South Car-
olina, some of the members decided to take an afternoon
off and relax at the beach. Everyone went for a swim, including Ray, who had learned to swim in Greenville
years before. The water was cool and refreshing, and Ray
kept swimming farther and farther out into the ocean.
Suddenly he heard one of the musicians yelling at him to
come back. Thinking his friend was worried he might
drown, Ray turned and swam back to shore. The others
told him he had turned back just in time. They explained

that the danger was not in swimming too far out, but in swimming too close to the beach's "white" side. Ray was bewildered by the peculiarities of racism. How could the ocean be divided into black and white? But as he continued to travel with his band, he grew increasingly aware of prejudice and bigotry. He learned about separate rest rooms, restaurants, and hotels for blacks and whites. The other musicians told him about signs that read, "No Jews, dogs, or niggers allowed." Ray realized that Jews and blacks were often lumped in the same category by bigots.

As he traveled all over the country, Ray grew more and more aware of racism.

He felt a kind of attachment to the Jews—they were also
victims of bigotry.

In 1951 Ray made a decision about his singing style.
For more than seven years,　he had admired the sophisticated sound of Nat Cole, who was now known as Nat

Nat "King" Cole

"King" Cole. For years Ray had tried to sound like Cole. When anyone told him that he did, he was delighted. Now it began to dawn on Ray that he should stop sounding like someone else. It was important to be original—to sound like himself. While he didn't give up imitations all at once, Ray began to concentrate on his own sound. He started to develop a throaty, soulful, singing voice filled with emotion.

In another move to assert his independence, Ray decided to arrange for his own transportation on the road. He bought a used car and hired a driver. Now when he traveled with Fulson, he could follow the other musicians in their van and play his radio as loud as he wanted without disturbing anyone. Ray enjoyed being on the move, but he liked to move his own way.

In 1952 Ray decided to go solo.

CHAPTER   NINE

HIS OWN
PERSON

RAY'S RELATIONSHIPS WITH WOMEN DID NOT usually last long. By 1952, he was no longer dating Loretta. One of Ray's musician friends, Billy Brooks, introduced him to a young woman named Eileen. Billy had recently married his longtime girlfriend. Suddenly the idea of marriage and a home also appealed to Ray. Though he had dated Eileen for only three weeks, Ray asked her to marry him.

They married and moved into their own apartment, but a couple of weeks after the wedding Ray had to go on the road. Traveling around the country to play gigs was an important part of Ray's life. Eileen had a job of her own as a successful beautician and couldn't follow her husband. Before long, the fragile relationship began to fall apart. Sixteen months later, the young couple divorced.

Ray decided it was time to leave the Lowell Fulson band and strike out on his own. He went to New York

and got involved with the Billy Shaw Agency, which became responsible for booking Ray's gigs. When Ray met
Billy Shaw, Shaw told the young musician something un-
settling. He explained that any time the Shaw Agency did
not fulfill its duties to Ray, Ray could leave the agency.
On the other hand, Shaw added, if Ray didn't meet his
duties for the agency, it would drop him. The rules of the
business world were new to Ray, but he realized that
Shaw was just being up front with him.

In 1952 Ray signed up to record his music with an outfit called Atlantic Records. For the next two years, Ray
toured on his own. He found it difficult to locate other
musicians to play the kind of gigs he liked—a combination
of jazz, swing, and blues. Sometimes he had to play with
whatever band happened to be available to back him up.
Ray liked his music to be played precisely, without
wrong notes or missed cues, and he got upset with careless
band members. He decided that if he had his own band,
he could impose his own kind of musical discipline, and
the music would sound the way he knew it should. Ray
called the Shaw Agency in New York and told them he
wanted to form his own band. Mr. Shaw pointed out that
having his own band would not mean an end to all of
Ray's problems, but Ray had made up his mind.

Slowly and carefully, Ray put together his first band. It
was not a big one, but Ray was proud of it. It consisted of
seven instrumentalists. David Newman played baritone
saxophone; Jimmy Bell played guitar; Bill Peeples played
drums; Joe Bridgewater and Clarky White played trumpet;

and a musician named A. D. played tenor saxophone. Ray played piano and wrote most of the arrangements. With Ray as the leader, each player gave his best performance, switching easily from jazz to rhythm and blues.

Ray began to create sounds that people told him were new and different. To Ray, his music was just his normal way of expressing himself. He had been listening to spirituals since he was three years old. Combining their haunting sound with the energetic sounds of blues and jazz seemed quite natural. He adapted a song originally called "You Better Leave That Liar Alone," and it became "You Better Leave That Woman Alone." Other tunes based on spirituals were "Lonely Avenue" and "Talkin' Bout You." Some of his songs were based on a combination of three or four gospel numbers.

This combination of gospel, blues, and jazz came from Ray's own background and experience. The result was natural, honest, and effortless. Ray knew he had developed a sound that belonged to him. From now on, no one could say he sounded like somebody else. Ray had dreams about the future, though he never discussed them with anyone. He liked to imagine that someday he would perform in a famous place like New York's Carnegie Hall.

Inspired because he had his own band, Ray started writing more original tunes. Atlantic Records encouraged him and recorded his songs without changing them. It was unusual for a young and inexperienced composer to receive this kind of cooperation from a recording company. Ray was delighted.

In 1953, in Texas for a gig, Ray met a singer named
Della. Della was a quiet, unassuming young woman who
didn't drink or smoke. She was also rather shy. Ray found
Della refreshingly different from other women he had
known. He was quickly drawn to the young singer. He
called her "B" for her middle name, Beatrice. Though he
had to leave for other gigs, he called and wrote letters,
and the romance blossomed. Ray soon convinced B to ac-
company him to Dallas. He had decided to be honest
about all his relationships. He told her about his ex-
sweetheart, Louise; his daughter, Evelyn; and his marriage to Eileen. Ray was anxious to make this relationship
work. His "other mother," Mary Jane, had recently passed
away, and the desire for family of his own was stronger
than ever.

In 1954 Ray and B were married and set up a home together in Dallas. A year later, while Ray was out of town
on a gig, his son Ray Jr. was born. When Ray came home
and realized how tiny the new baby was, he was almost
afraid to hold him. But that fear didn't last long. By the
time little Ray was a few months old, his father took great
pleasure in playing with him. Unfortunately, Ray wasn't
home often enough to spend much time with his wife
and child. Though she was busy with her small son, B
missed Ray when he had to leave for his gigs.

When they were first married, B didn't know about
Ray's drug problem. He had told her about his past rela-
tionships, but he wanted to keep his addiction a secret.
One morning, however, Ray left a cotton ball lying in a

burnt spoon in the bathroom. B recognized these objects as materials for using heroin. She was very unhappy and didn't know how to deal with the situation. Though she was upset, she tried not to pressure her husband.

By 1955 Ray Charles had become a confident, well-organized bandleader. Using the same kind of discipline

Ray leads his band in rehearsal.

Mama had taught him, he urged his players to always give
their best. He worked hard and insisted that they work
hard, too. The musicians respected Ray, and the band
played well together. They performed in many well-known
black theaters, including the Apollo in New York, the Re-
gal in Chicago, the Howard in Washington, D.C., and the
Royal in Baltimore. Most of the time they performed for
black audiences.

Fans stand in line for tickets at the Apollo Theater.

Traveling through the Southern states, Ray and his band experienced a number of unpleasant encounters with racial prejudice. Because they were often unable to find a gas station that would allow them to use the washroom, they had to relieve themselves by hiding behind the open doors of their car.

When it came to professional situations, Ray refused to accept the so-called "rules" of segregation. In Augusta, Georgia, the owner of a theater told Ray that the black audience would be seated upstairs and the white audience downstairs. Ray responded by saying he wanted it the other way around. As a black person who had always been supported by black people, Ray had no intention of insulting the black audience that had come out expressly to see him. If the seating arrangements were not changed, Ray said, he and the band would not perform. The theater owner threatened to sue Ray, and he did. He went to court and the case cost Ray more than two thousand dollars. But Ray was not sorry he had stood by his beliefs. In Nashville, Tennessee, Ray once again refused to play to a segregated audience. This time, the theater owner agreed to Ray's conditions.

In 1955, while performing in Kentucky, Ray heard Mary Ann Fisher, a singer whose style he liked. He offered Mary Ann an opportunity to sing with the band. Her sentimental ballads gave Ray's band a new touch. They also gave Ray a new idea. He had always enjoyed the sound of women's voices in gospel choirs. Now he started to think about adding a strong female backup group as a contrast to his own voice.

Two years later, while in Philadelphia, Ray heard a trio of female vocalists he thought would be perfect. They called themselves the Cookies. He convinced them to work with him. Ray changed their name to the Raeletts and wrote brand-new arrangements for them. For a while, Mary Ann Fisher stayed on as the fourth Raelett.

With the addition of the Raeletts, Ray's band had grown to 11 members. Ray was pleased with the new vocalists, but he soon became aware of an unexpected problem. For the first time, women had become a regular part of the organization. While Ray realized that his band members were all adults and he didn't have a right to interfere with their private lives, he decided he would still have to lay down a few ground rules to prevent uncomfortable situations. There were to be no physical fights; singing came before anything else; and the men had to stay away from the youngest Raelett, Pat, because she was only 15 years old. Other than these three rules, Ray let them all be who they wanted to be.

Soon after the Raeletts joined the band, the number of gigs began to increase considerably. Ray recorded several popular hits. Atlantic Records was becoming a leader in the recording industry, and Ray was glad to be working with them. Among the new records were "I Got a Woman," "A Fool for You," "Drown in My Own Tears," and "Hallelujah, I Love Her So."

Band members told Ray that more and more white people were showing up at performances. Though Ray was glad that his music was becoming more popular with more people, he did not change his writing or his playing to appeal to the white crowd.

In 1958 Ray's second son, David, was born. Ray was delighted, but he still couldn't spend much time at home. B couldn't travel with small children, so once again the family was separated. A few months later, Ray bought a house in Los Angeles and moved his family there. The weather was better than in Dallas, but unfortunately, everything else remained the same. Ray still had to be on the road most of the time. He invited B to come with him, but she loved her little boys and didn't want anyone else to raise them. So B stayed home, and Ray went out to pursue the career that meant more to him than anything else in the world.

Ray proudly accepts the audience's applause.

FREEDOM

IN 1959 RAY CHARLES ACHIEVED HIS LONGTIME dream of appearing at Carnegie Hall. When the time came to go on stage, he was surprised to find he wasn't nervous. He was excited to be on the same bill with Billie Holiday, the popular singer he had always admired but never met. Though Lady Day was ill, she put on a wonderful show, and Ray admired her professional attitude.

In 1960 Ray appeared on national television with celebrities Dinah Shore and Ed Sullivan. He also traveled to Europe for the first time. Flying was Ray's favorite method of transportation. Now that he was making money, he bought his own plane—a small twin-engine Cessna 310. Ray loved to sit beside the pilot, listening to every sound and sometimes handling the controls.

Ray formed a private music publishing company in 1961, calling it Tangerine—his favorite fruit. Now Ray had the freedom to record and publish anything he wanted. One of the songs he recorded was a romantic melody, "Georgia on My Mind." Some listeners believed he was singing about a lady called Georgia. Ray didn't

Ray gives an interview in 1962.

have either the state or a lady in mind, he just liked the
sound. The song became a big hit. Ray developed a number of original musical concepts, among them songs with
women's names. "Ruby" became a big seller. Another,
though not original, was "Nancy," a song Ray had always
wanted to record. "Dinah" was another hit.

In 1961 Ray's third son, Bobby, was born. Wanting a
nice home for his growing family, Ray bought property to

build a house in an upper-class black neighborhood of Los Angeles. B did most of the planning and soon the family had a comfortable split-level house with plenty of land for the kids to play on. At around the same time, Ray's new recording studio, R.P.M. (Records, Publishing, and Management) International, moved into a two-story building between Beverly Hills and the Watts neighborhood of Los Angeles. Joe Adams, a longtime friend who had been a disc jockey with station KOWL, became Ray's manager and handled the business side of R.P.M.

In 1962 Ray experimented with country-and-western music. Ray had never tried this style of singing on his own, and some of his friends warned him that branching into country music might injure his expanding career. Country music attracted a mostly white audience, and Ray's friends told him that he might even lose his black fans. But Ray was intent on trying his wings with "hillbilly" music. He'd admired the music of the Grand Ole Opry—a radio program based in Nashville—since he was a kid in the Florida countryside.

Ray put out an album called *Modern Sounds in Country and Western Music.* He put his own spin on country songs. The success of songs such as "I Can't Stop Loving You," "You Are My Sunshine," and "You Don't Know Me" gave him larger white audiences than black.

When Ray started recording country songs, he was faulted by black critics for combining black music with white. These objections didn't bother Ray. He figured people would buy the music they liked to listen to, no

Ray was confident that he could successfully sing country-and-western music as well as the blues, jazz, and soul music.

Ray played himself in the movie Ballad in Blue.

matter what style it was based on. He also did not believe he would lose black fans, only gain more white ones.

In the spring of 1964, Ray traveled to England and Ireland, where he played himself in the movie *Ballad in Blue,* the story of a blind boy with an overprotective mother. In the movie, Ray persuades the boy's mother to let her son be more independent. Ray also recorded some songs for the film's soundtrack, including the title song.

Ray adjusts the sound for a recording.

The same year, Ray and his band gave a successful concert in the Shrine Auditorium in Los Angeles. At the end of 1964, Ray and his group flew to Canada to play a gig. Their return flight landed at Logan International Airport in Boston.

From Logan, Ray and the other musicians were driven to their hotel. No sooner did Ray get into his room than he realized he had left a package of heroin on the plane. Immediately, he had himself driven back to the plane. He was relieved to find the package where he had left it, and he put it carefully in his coat pocket. Before he could step back into the car, he was stopped by a federal narcotics agent. The agent told Ray that the Federal Bureau of Investigation (FBI) had received a tip that the singer was carrying drugs. The agent asked him to hand over his coat. Ray was then arrested for narcotics possession and taken to court. Ray pleaded guilty. A year would pass before Ray's sentencing, so the singer canceled his tour and went home to California. He had a lot of thinking to do.

The following spring, Ray was invited to sing the title song of a movie called *The Cincinnati Kid*. Arrangements were made to record on a Thursday night at RCA studios. But ten-year-old Ray Jr. invited his father to a Little League banquet on the same night. The boy was receiving a trophy and wanted both of his parents to be there. Ray immediately called RCA and asked for a postponement. The studio agreed to put the recording session off for a week. A few hours later, however, Ray's son learned that the Little League dinner had also been postponed for one week.

Because Ray had promised, he went to the banquet with his wife and son. As dinner got under way, Ray started getting nervous. The trophy presentation would be made after the meal, and now it was almost 7:30.

Ray often put his performing career before his family.

Eight o'clock came and went, and Ray Jr. had not yet received his trophy. His troubled father leaned over and whispered that he had to leave. When his son began to cry, Ray thought his heart would break, but he tore himself away.

But Ray couldn't shut out the sound of his son's tears. He heard them all through his recording session, and even afterward. He realized how important being a father really was. He understood that if he ever had to spend time in jail because of his drug habit, he would destroy the already weak relationship he had with his son.

At that moment, Ray made one of the most important decisions his life. No matter what it took, he was determined to get rid of his drug addiction once and for all. He never wanted to worry that his son would be ashamed or hurt because of him.

In August 1965, Ray checked himself into St. Francis Hospital outside of Los Angeles. Ray refused the usual treatment for narcotics withdrawal. He would not take pills, sedatives, or tranquilizers to ease the difficulty of withdrawal.

For the first few days he was very sick, but he had promised himself he was going to make it on his own. He stayed in his room and concentrated on overcoming the pain and misery with every bit of willpower he could collect. Not convinced that Ray was seriously going "cold turkey"—withdrawing from narcotics suddenly and completely—hospital employees searched Ray's room and belongings. They could not find drugs hidden anywhere.

Finally, they gave him several tests that proved he was clean. Ray had broken a 17-year addiction.

Staying in the hospital was not easy for Ray. He was not used to inactivity. He did learn to play chess, which made the time go more quickly. B also came to visit, which helped a great deal. At night, playing cards and drinking tea with the nurses made the hours move a little faster.

Ray's lawyers told him that if he cooperated with the judge at the drug sentencing, he might stand a better chance. They meant that to receive a lighter sentence, Ray should name the person who sold him the drugs. Ray refused. After leaving the hospital, he returned to Boston to be sentenced. Ray's psychiatrist from St. Francis testified that the singer was free of narcotics addiction. But Ray knew he could still be sent to another hospital or to prison. When the judge reviewed the case, he postponed sentencing for another year and placed Ray on probation. For the next year, Ray would report to a probation officer and also to a hospital for further drug tests to be certain he stayed clean. Ray did not go back on the road for the rest of that year.

When the year was up, Ray again returned to Boston for sentencing. He learned that the original judge had died. The new judge had a reputation for being very tough. Just before the hearing, the judge opened a sealed envelope. It contained a note from the previous judge, who said that society would be better off with Ray Charles free, serving as a good example of a guy who kicked drugs, instead of ending up in prison.

The second judge agreed. He did not give Ray a prison sentence. Instead he placed him on five years probation. Ray Charles was free at last, not only to do his own thing in the world of music, but also to serve as the good example the judge had wisely proclaimed he would be.

Ray Charles leaves the courtroom a free man.

GENIUS OF SOUL

WHEN RAY RETURNED TO THE ROAD IN 1966, A few critics made negative comments about his drug arrest. Yet the crowds at his performances were as large as they had ever been. "Crying Time," a song he had composed during his year of probation, became a big hit. Ray was credited with inventing the sound known as "soul," but he refused to take credit for it. He believed that "soul" was just the way black singers expressed themselves.

Ray was not particularly fond of rock music. He thought it was too unstructured and disorderly. Other than rock, however, there were few kinds of music that he wouldn't try.

In the 1950s and 1960s, civil rights groups were working to combat racial oppression and injustice. When Ray went to Alabama to play at a civil rights benefit, he met Martin Luther King Jr., a black leader who believed nonviolence was the best way to cope with acts of bigotry and

Martin Luther King Jr. speaks out against discrimination.

prejudice. Ray admired King for his courage, but when it came to marching in protest, Ray did not join him. He didn't feel like he would be capable of the passive resistance favored by King and his followers. If someone hit Ray, he believed he'd have to hit back.

Ray played his music all over the world in the 1960s. Audiences in Europe, Asia, South America, North Africa, New Zealand, and Japan responded warmly to his unique

style and sound. Audiences around the world were capti-
vated by Ray's voice: rich, powerful, and raw with feeling. In his travels, Ray enjoyed listening to the music of
other cultures.

The Raeletts' sweet voices contrast with Ray's deep, chesty tone.

In Great Britain, Ray received reactions he did not expect. He had been told by other entertainers that English
people were cold spectators who were slow to respond. As
a result, the singer postponed going to England. Yet when
Ray finally made an appearance in England, he was pleas-
antly surprised by the British fans' love and appreciation.

In countries such as Hungary, Bulgaria, and Yugo-
slavia, people reacted to the blind singer as if he were a
dear long-lost relation. To Ray's surprise, the country in
which he received the most standing ovations was Israel,
the Jewish homeland. At a concert in Jerusalem, where he
had been scheduled to give two performances, the first
crowd became so enthusiastic they would not leave. The
concert hall manager didn't know what to do. Ray suggested that people could stay for the second show if they
gave up their seats. The announcement was greeted with
cheers of approval. During the second show, people
crowded in the aisles.

Ray was particularly thrilled to meet Israel's prime
minister, David Ben-Gurion. When Ray arrived, Ben-
Gurion invited him to the kibbutz, or communal farm,
where he lived. The two men had dinner and talked for
hours. Ben-Gurion showed Ray around the kibbutz and
explained how it worked. Ray enjoyed talking with the
kibbutz residents and learning more about them. By the
time he left Israel, he felt a great deal of respect for its
people and their will to survive despite major obstacles.

Although he experienced professional success, Ray
had troubles at home. In 1976, B filed for a legal separa-

Ray plays to the audience.

tion. Ray was unhappy and agreed to go with B to a marriage counselor to try to salvage their marriage, but this didn't help. He admitted that he was too preoccupied with making music and money to have a normal home life. In 1977, B and Ray divorced. It hurt Ray to realize he did not have the traits necessary to be a devoted husband and father.

After the divorce, Ray tried to maintain a relationship with his ex-wife and three sons. Whenever B needed help or advice with anything, Ray made a sincere effort to be there for her. When B's mother passed away, Ray rode with B in the family car, holding her hand and comforting her. When Ray had a birthday, B would make a family party with homemade pound cake and ice cream. The boys enjoyed helping their father celebrate.

In the years that followed, Ray continued to have romantic encounters with women who attracted him. He never allowed these relationships to become too serious, however. He did not want to marry again. Writing songs, recording arrangements, and traveling around the world with his band kept him as busy as he liked to be. Using his private plane, he could cover 400 miles in an hour to get to one of his concerts. Remembering long, hot trips in the backs of crowded buses, Ray enjoyed air travel.

In 1979 the Georgia state legislature made Ray's version of "Georgia on My Mind" the official state song. Ray was invited to Atlanta to perform in the House of Representatives. Ray was deeply touched. In the following years, he received awards from various governments, cities, schools, and organizations. In 1983 he was honored with the NAACP (National Association for the Advancement of Colored People) Hall of Fame Award. The award that impressed him the most was the B'nai B'rith (a Jewish organization) Man of the Year award, which he received at a banquet in Los Angeles. Composer Sammy Cahn sang special songs in Ray's honor.

In 1986 Ray became ill with an inner ear infection that caused not only pain but also serious concern. Ray worried that if he lost his hearing, he would lose his music. Fortunately, Ray received medical treatment that cured the infection and restored his hearing. Soon after, Ray continued to travel the globe with his band and the Raeletts. Some of the original Raeletts left the band and were replaced by other female singers, and Ray continued to enjoy the tone of women's voices contrasting with his own special sound.

In 1986 Ray became one of the original inductees into the Rock 'n' Roll Hall of Fame. He was also a Kennedy Center honoree along with celebrities Lucille Ball, Yehudi Menuhin, Hume Cronyn, and Jessica Tandy. President Ronald Reagan hung a medal around Ray's neck as millions watched on national television. In 1988, having received 11 Grammy Awards during his career, Ray received the Grammy Lifetime Achievement Award.

Always interested in experimenting with new musical forms, Ray teamed up with choreographer Peter Martins

The 1986 Kennedy Center honorees were, clockwise from upper left, *Ray Charles, Antony Tudor, Yehudi Menuhin, Lucille Ball, Hume Cronyn, and Jessica Tandy.*

to produce a ballet set to a Ray Charles tune called "A Fool for You." The ballet had its world premiere in 1988 during the American Music Festival.

Ray also continued to appear in films and on television. He acted in a movie called *The Blues Brothers,* as well as on the television shows *St. Elsewhere* and *Who's the Boss.* When the hit celebrity charity anthem, "We Are the World" was recorded, Ray led the final chorus.

Ray is an active humanitarian, contributing to civil rights causes, African famine relief, and organizations that help the hearing impaired. In 1987 he began the Robinson Foundation for Hearing Disorders with an endowment of one million dollars. In 1990 Ray was honored in a gala celebration marking his 60th birthday and

Ray sings with his band and the Raeletts.

Ray plays a music store owner in The Blues Brothers *with Dan Aykroyd,* left, *and John Belushi.*

45th year in show business. The party was hosted by Ear International, a support organization for the hearing impaired, at the Bel Air Hotel in Los Angeles. The gala was the organization's way of saying thank-you to Ray for the fund-raisers he had successfully completed in the past. For his part, the singer believes that "most people take their ears for granted. I can't. My eyes are my handicap, but my ears are my opportunity."

Uh-huh! Diet Pepsi's TV commercial

Ray continues to record and to play at benefits. He makes a lot of TV commercials. His campaign for Diet Pepsi, with its catchy refrain, "You got the right one, baby, uh-huh!" was rated the most memorable commercial of 1991. He travels nine months of the year with his musicians and the Raeletts, performing with the same energy

Musicians join the audience in applauding Stevie Wonder and Ray Charles.

and excitement he did 30 years ago. When he is away from the road, Ray doesn't socialize much. He has an apartment in Beverly Hills but spends much of his time in the recording studio, surrounded by the instruments he loves.

Ray in his element—singing

Ray's hair is silver-gray now, but his body is as lean and broad-shouldered as when he first started performing. He rocks back and forth when he sings and reaches out to his fans when he is touched. He wears the trademark wrap-around dark glasses. The voice is chesty and powerful, sometimes chuckling, sometimes groaning and crying as the lyrics and music come together.

A few years ago when Ray was asked if he had plans to retire, his answer left no room for doubt:

> Music to me is part of me. I am never going to retire from it. I would play music for nothing. I look at music the same as I look at my bloodstream, my respiratory system, my lungs. It's something I have to have.

Among the titles that have been bestowed on the singer in recent years are "the father of soul music," "the greatest pop singer of his generation, "a true American musical original," and most recently, "the genius of soul." On hearing this glowing praise, Ray Charles unabashedly rejects it. He claims, "I have sense enough to know I am not a genius."

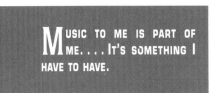

MUSIC TO ME IS PART OF ME. . . . IT'S SOMETHING I HAVE TO HAVE.

In a fitting tribute, President Bill Clinton awarded Ray the National Medal of Arts in a ceremony on the south lawn of the White House on October 8, 1993. Among some of the other distinguished Americans to be recognized for their contributions to the arts and humanities that day were bandleader Cab Calloway and playwright Arthur Miller.

Today, the world of modern music continues to claim Ray Charles as the genius of his particular sound. By fusing the magnetic sounds of gospel, jazz, blues, and country-and-western music, Ray Charles has played a major role in charting new horizons and influencing generations of musicians around the world.

Rising above poverty, prejudice, blindness, and drug addiction, the singer-composer has turned his unique talent into a passionate celebration of the black American experience.

D I S C O G R A P H Y

A small selection of Ray Charles's many albums:

On Atlantic records:

Hallelujah, I Love Her So
Yes Indeed
What I Say
The Genius of Ray Charles
The Genius After Hours
The Genius Sings the Blues
Ray Charles, Live
The Ray Charles Story
Soul Meeting

On ABC records:

Genius Hits the Road
Modern Sounds in Country and Western Music
Country & Western Music Meets Rhythm and Blues
Crying Time
A Portrait of Ray
I'm All Yours, Baby
Doing His Thing
Volcanic Action of My Soul
Through the Eyes of Love

On Tangerine records:

Ray Charles Presents the Raeletts, Yesterday . . . Today . . .
  Tomorrow

On Crossover records:

Come Live with Me
Renaissance

On Columbia records:

Wish You Were here Tonight
Do I Ever Cross Your Mind?
From the Pages of My Mind
Just Between Us

On Warner records:

Would You Believe?

Ray Charles on video:

We Are the World: The Video Event
Ray Charles: The Genius of Soul
Ray Charles Live 1991: A Romantic Evening at the McCallum
  Theater

S O U R C E S

Quotes on the following pages are
reprinted from:

24   Ray Charles and David Ritz,
     *Brother Ray: Ray Charles' Own
     Story* (New York: Da Capo
     Press, 1992), 17.

26   Louie Robinson, "The Enduring
     Genius of Ray Charles: From
     Folk to Rock, Most Artists Owe
     a Debt to Multi-Talented
     Musician," *Ebony,* October
     1974.

45   Interview with John Morthland,
     New York Newsday, 22 May 83.

100   *Current Biography Yearbook*
      (New York: H. W. Wilson, 1992),
      119.

102   Diet Pepsi commercial, 1991.

104   Jacqueline Trescott, "Ray
      Charles, Amen!: Soul's Survivor
      and His Song of Contentment,"
      Washington Post, 21 May 1980.

104   Ibid.

P H O T O   A C K N O W L E D G M E N T S

The photographs have been reproduced by permission of: Archive
Photos, pp. 1, 19, 58, 63, 74, 78, 80, 84, 86, 89, 93, 99; AP, p. 2; IPS,
Nancy Smedstad, p. 6; Library of Congress, p. 9; The Maitland Art
Center, p. 10; UPI/Bettmann, pp. 11, 52, 66, 73, 92; Florida State
Archives, pp. 14, 18, 22, 31, 36; Archive Photos/Frank Driggs
Collection, pp. 25, 32, 40; National Archives, p. 28 (#Am Im 180);
Hollywood Book and Poster, pp. 43, 46, 55, 68, 100, 101; Seattle
Post—Intelligencer Collection, Museum of History and Industry, pp.
50, 54; Greater Los Angeles Convention and Visitor's Bureau, p. 61;
Schomburg Center for Research in Black Culture, p. 65; Photofest, pp.
82, 83, 90, 105, 106; Wide World Photos, Inc., pp. 95, 98, 102, 103.

Front and back cover photos used by permission of Photofest.

BIBLIOGRAPHY

Balliet, Whitney. *American Singers: Twenty-Seven Portraits in Song.* New York: Oxford University Press, 1979.

Charles, Ray, and David Ritz. *Brother Ray: Ray Charles' Own Story.* New York: Da Capo Press, 1992.

Feather, Leonard. *From Satchmo to Miles.* New York: Da Capo Press, 1972.

Fong-Torres, Ben. "Ray Charles." *Rolling Stone,* 15 October 1992.

Goldberg, Joe. *Jazz Masters of the Fifties.* New York: Macmillan, 1965.

Lydon, Michael. "Raw Truth and Joy: Ray Charles Cuts Through His Smoothness with Jolts of Musical Pleasure." *Atlantic,* March 1991.

Palmer, Robert. "Soul Survivor Ray Charles." *Rolling Stone,* 9 February 1978.

Robinson, Louie. "The Enduring Genius of Ray Charles: From Folk to Rock, Most Artists Owe a Debt to Multi-Talented Musician." *Ebony,* October 1974.

Shaw, Arnold. *Black Popular Music in America.* New York: Schirmer Books, 1986.

Trescott, Jacqueline. "Ray Charles, Amen!: Soul's Survivor and His Song of Contentment." *Washington Post.* 21 May 1980.

112

ABOUT THE AUTHOR

Ruth Turk—author, lecturer, columnist, and teacher—has been writing since the age of nine. Her first poem was published in the *New York Times* when she was 10. Since then, she has written books for both children and adults on a wide range of topics. Her biography entitled *Lillian Hellman: Rebel Playwright* was also published by Lerner Publications. She has been a teacher of elementary, junior high, and high school students. Ruth and her husband live in Florida.

Lerner's **Newsmakers** series:
Muhammad Ali: Champion
Ray Charles: Soul Man
The 14th Dalai Lama: Spiritual Leader of Tibet
Sir Edmund Hillary: To Everest and Beyond